CORINNE NOBLE

SPARK

A Creative Take on Kids Ministry

Spark: A Creative Take on Kids Ministry
by Corinne Noble

copyright ©2019 Corinne Noble
cover design by Kiryl Lisenko

ISBN: 978-1-950718-01-6

Scripture marked MSG taken from The Message. Copyright © 1993, 1994, 1995, 1996, 2000, 2001, 2002. Used by permission of NavPress Publishing Group.

Scripture marked ESV taken from ESV® Bible (The Holy Bible, English Standard Version®), copyright © 2001 by Crossway, a publishing ministry of Good News Publishers. Used by permission. All rights reserved."

Scripture marked NIV taken from THE HOLY BIBLE, NEW INTERNATIONAL VERSION®, NIV® Copyright © 1973, 1978, 1984, 2011 by Biblica, Inc.® Used by permission. All rights reserved worldwide.

Scripture marked AMP taken from Amplified® Bible (AMP), Copyright © 2015 by The Lockman Foundation, Used by permission. www.Lockman.org

Scripture marked CSB taken from The Christian Standard Bible. Copyright © 2017 by Holman Bible Publishers. Used by permission. Christian Standard Bible®, and CSB® are federally registered trademarks of Holman Bible Publishers, all rights reserved.

Scripture marked NKJV taken from the New King James Version®. Copyright © 1982 by Thomas Nelson. Used by permission. All rights reserved.

CONTENTS

INTRODUCTION 5
1. WHY CREATIVITY IS ESSENTIAL 7
2. HELP! I'M NOT CREATIVE 13
3. INVITING ENVIRONMENTS 21
4. GIVING YOUR ENVIRONMENTS A FRESH LOOK 27
5. ENVIRONMENTS ON A BUDGET 37
6. STRATEGIC EVENTS 47
7. MAKE VBS GREAT AGAIN 55
8. HOW TO CHOOSE THE BEST GAMES 65
9. OBJECT LESSONS OUT OF ANYTHING 73
10. HOW TO CHOOSE THE RIGHT CURRICULUM 79
11. CREATING YOUR OWN CURRICULUM 87
FINAL THOUGHTS 95

INTRODUCTION

I'M SO GLAD YOU DECIDED to pick up this book. It doesn't matter if you are a die-hard creative from birth, a learned creative, or a person who doesn't think you have a creative bone in your body, this book is for you. Kids ministry is filled with opportunities to grow your creativity. What other ministry position is expected to organize volunteers, plan entire services, preach sermons, direct major events, and decorate environments? I'm convinced you can't be in kids ministry for long without creativity and a whole lot of Jesus! Creativity should be in the job description.

You will learn that creativity is essential in every aspect of your life and ministry. If you feel like you aren't the most creative person in the world, that's ok. This book will help you fix your creativity void. We will look at some of the key areas that require creativity in your ministry. These chapters will cover environments, events, games, object lessons, and curriculum. I'm certain there will be chapters that make you feel like a boss because you are already rocking it in that area of your ministry. There will likely be other chapters that will challenge you to step up your game or change it up for the first time in decades.

Creativity often involves trying new things and being willing to fail. Don't be afraid of change, but don't try to change everything all at once. Make a list of the areas you would like to modify and rank them by importance. Start with the most important area, cast vision to your pastor, your team, and the families in your ministry, then start making some changes. There isn't one right way to do kids ministry; you can make it your own. As long as you keep Christ at the center of everything you do, you will start to feel the creative juices flowing.

There is one important thing I always do before I begin any project: I pray. Before I began writing this book, I prayed and asked God to give me the clarity, courage, and creativity to share these ideas with all of you. Why? Because I never want to think I'm doing this on my own. I pray that God would be glorified through every word. I also pray that many kids will be drawn to your churches and come to know Jesus as their personal Savior because of the God-given creative ideas you put into action in your kids ministries. Before you begin reading each chapter, I want to encourage you to pray and ask God what He wants to reveal to you about your creativity.

chapter 1

WHY CREATIVITY IS ESSENTIAL

Look around you! Creativity is everywhere you look. What would life be without it? Take a walk outside, and it won't take long for you to become inspired by the creativity you see in nature all around you. You can't help but think creatively when you're outside. I was walking around my neighborhood a few days ago enjoying the breeze, and I looked down at the rocks in the yards. Lots of tiny rocks made up each yard. I picked up a few of these tiny rocks and began to look at the detail in each rock. None of them were the same.

Our amazing God created everything with such detail, including each one of us. We were made by the most creative Creator of all time. When we look to God's Word, the first thing we see is creativity. In the beginning, there was nothing before creativity took place. Without creativity, nothing would exist. You can't get a lot more essential than that. Can you imagine if God had decided to only create one kind of plant? We would be eating nothing but kale for the rest of our lives! What if He had decided to only make one kind of animal? Our pets would also be what's for dinner. What if every human being looked exactly the same, had the same hair color, eye color, skin color, height, and weight? Life would be plain boring and confusing without the detail that we see in creation.

Creativity is not limited to nature. God created each of us with that same ability to create something new out of nothing. Creativity takes an idea that is ordinary and makes it extraordinary. Think of the most creative place you have ever seen. Maybe you thought of a place that is filled with nature like the Grand Canyon, or maybe you thought of a place that was man-made, like Disneyland?

The best places in the world are places where creativity is most evident. What is the difference between amusement parks like Six Flags and Disneyland? At Six Flags, you can ride roller coasters and have a great time, but at Disneyland, everything is an experience. There were amusement parks in existence before Walt Disney decided to create Disneyland, but none of them had exactly what he was looking for. He wanted to take the same imagination and creativity found in the movies that children and families loved come to life in a place they could experience together. Disney didn't let anything stop him from creating an unforgettable experience for families. For example, he wanted to have real animals on the Jungle Cruise, but zoologists told him that was impossible. He could have scrapped the Jungle Cruise idea altogether, but instead he put on his creativity cap. He loved using technology and had his team create robotic animals to inhabit the Jungle Cruise. He was a problem solver who never let anything stand in his way. Six Flags may be great, but Disneyland is next-level creativity.

Another example I can think of is the difference between an ordinary hotel and the Gaylord hotels. When I lived in Texas a few years ago, I loved going to the Gaylord Texan Hotel, especially around Christmas time. Many people would go there

Why Creativity Is Essential

even if they weren't staying at the hotel overnight. There are trees, restaurants, shops, and water features inside the hotel. It's like you are stepping into another world, and you can almost forget you are inside a building. During the Christmas season, they even create an indoor winter wonderland experience called Ice! They take millions of pounds of ice, then transform it into slides and create an entire storyline of a beloved Christmas story using only ice.

Talk about thinking big and maybe a little crazy! However, it's fun and unique and as a result, millions of kids and parents come each year to experience the new theme. Both Disneyland and the Gaylord Texan Hotel have one thing in common: they are an experience that took something ordinary and brought it to another level through someone's creativity. I don't know about you, but I would rather be a part of a next-level experience any day over an ordinary experience, and I would guess the kids in our ministries would agree.

Now, let's take all of this and apply it to your kids ministry. Close your eyes and imagine your ministry for a moment. Begin to think through all the different aspects. What is a child or family going to see when they walk into your church for the first time? How is that first impression going to reflect on your ministry and the church as a whole? What events are coming up in the next few months? Are they engaging and exciting, or are they the same old overdone events?

Next, take a look at your services. Have you been playing the same large group game for the last five months? How are you making the Bible come to life right before your kids' eyes and helping them apply it to their daily lives? What about the curriculum you are using? That's a big one! Are you simply using the same curriculum just because it's what you have always done or because it fits your budget? Do you see your volunteers holding a sheet of paper, reading from it, or are they engaging the kids by looking them in the eye and making it their own?

Spark

I hope you really will take a good hard look at where your ministry is right now. I'm sure as you think about it, there are areas of your ministry that you feel good about, and there are areas that could use a bit of a facelift. I know we all have to wear a lot of hats in our ministries, and I'm not saying you should personally be amazing at everything. If every aspect of your ministry is already perfect, you can probably go ahead and put this book down, but who are we kidding? All of our ministries need some work and a little bit of creativity. In fact, creativity is all about keeping things fresh, new, and exciting. That means we all need to be constantly evaluating our ministries to keep things up to date.

Now, I don't know what all of you envisioned when you closed your eyes and imagined your kids ministry, but let's have some fun. I want us all to tap into our creativity and imagine all those areas again, but with a creative take on each one. Imagine a brand-new family stepping into your ministry environments for the first time to see fun decorations that go along with your theme and the creative use of projection and lighting that make them feel like they have just stepped into another world.

Next, imagine them making comments like, "This room reminds me of Disneyland!" That can really happen, even on a budget! Think of the events you have coming up and imagine kids actually getting excited about it and begging their parents to get them registered. Or, imagine it's time for service, and the kids can't wait to see what the game is going to be! It's never the same old game because you have taken the time to tie it into the theme, verse, or message of the day. You have taken the time to come up with and practice an object lesson that is going to blow their minds and keep them on the edge of their seats. You've found a curriculum that's a great fit for your kids, but you never use it the way it comes. You are always looking for ways to personalize it and make it relevant for the kids in your ministry. Maybe you've even

Why Creativity Is Essential

given creating your own curriculum a try. You keep hearing the kids talk about the latest video game, and you know you could create a fun curriculum the kids would love and be engaged in because it's exactly what they are into right now.

That all sounds amazing, right? That's what creativity can do for every aspect of your ministry. Creativity is the use of the imagination or original ideas to produce something. It's all about looking at things you always do from a new and fresh perspective to help you solve problems a different way. Creativity sometimes requires taking risks and trying something totally new that may even fail. That's a risk you should always be willing to take, because creativity can take your normal Sunday services and make them extraordinary. If you want kids and families attracted to and engaged by your ministry, creativity is an essential tool you need to learn how to leverage. We can't allow the world to own all the best experiences because we are too stuck in a comfortable routine. In the later chapters of this book, we will begin to dig deeper into some of the main areas of your ministry, and you will learn how to get a creative take on each one.

CREATIVITY CHALLENGE

Write down the three most creative places you can think of within driving distance of you. Make plans to go visit at least one of those places to look for inspiration. When you go, bring a notepad or take notes on your phone of ideas that come to you during your visit.

_____
_____
_____
_____
_____
_____
_____
_____
_____
_____
_____
_____
_____
_____
_____
_____
_____
_____
_____
_____
_____
_____
_____
_____
_____

chapter 2

HELP! I'M NOT CREATIVE

I CAN ALREADY HEAR SOME of you saying to yourselves, "But I'm just not creative." I used to say the exact same thing all the time. Since I was a little kid, I never fit the creative stereotype. While other kids were using Legos and blocks to create anything they could imagine, I would just sort them by shape and color. I had no interest or understanding of games that required you to use your imagination. I remember one time in fifth grade, I had to take an art class in school. I dreaded art class so much because I worked really hard at drawing a boat, but everyone said it looked like a shoe. I remember thinking to myself, "This is just not my thing. I'm not creative!"

Even after I received my calling to kids ministry, I never thought of myself as creative. Fast forward to a few years of working full time in kids ministry, and I have realized I can do so many things I never thought I could do before. I have come to realize that while I am still organized and a bit of a Type-A personality, I am also creative. I went from someone who used to say that I wasn't creative at all to being told by people that I'm the most creative person they have ever met. Now, I don't say that to toot my own horn, but I am telling you all of this because I want you to understand where I came from in my journey. I hope and pray that through hearing the story of someone who believed they weren't creative and discovered their inner creativity, you will realize you may have some creativity deep down inside after all. You simply need to find it!

I believe that we all have a stereotype of what it means to be creative in our minds. Maybe you envision a kid who could draw almost anything when they were only ten years old. Maybe you think of someone who is late, disorganized, and procrastinates, but they always manage to create something awesome on the fly. We need to stop putting creativity in a box. The very definition of creativity states that it cannot be contained. Creativity is going to look different for every person. Just because you can't draw a stick figure well doesn't mean you aren't creative, it just means you may not be a very good artist, but art is not the only form creativity can take. I believe the first step to finding your creativity is to stop saying you're not creative. Words have so much power, especially the words we speak to ourselves. When you keep saying something about yourself, regardless of whether it is negative or positive, you begin to believe it and accept it as the truth. Instead of saying to yourself, "I'm not creative," maybe try saying, "I'm finding my creativity."

The next step to finding your creativity is being open to new creative outlets! Try something new you have never tried before or retry something you tried a long time ago. Just because you were not good at something in the past doesn't mean that God won't give you the ability to excel at it now. I believe that God gives us new gifts for different seasons of life and ministry, if we are open to receiving them. In my first ministry job, I learned the importance of having a team of people with different gifts and abilities. Even if I could do everything on my own, I couldn't be omnipresent, and I was quickly exhausted trying

Help! I'm Not Creative

to do it all. I learned that I loved trying new things and putting together events for the kids and families in my ministry.

At my second ministry job, there was a lot of pressure on me to perform at a level I had never experienced before. I worked two or three times as hard as I did at my first position, but that pressure forced me to try new things. I continued to grow in my ability to plan events of all sizes, and I began to get into set design. I would typically complete at least one set design, and two or three events, each month. This went on for almost three years, and while those years were hard and exceptionally busy, I grew in ways I never thought possible and learned I was capable of so much more. The girl who couldn't even draw a recognizable boat was now designing stages!

In my third ministry position, I continued to use what I learned about events and set design, but I am much wiser about not running myself into the ground trying to do too many things. Just over two years ago, God showed me another area of creativity where He wanted to stretch and use my gift. I remember telling my assistant at the time only months earlier that I would never write my own kids ministry curriculum. It was just too hard, too much work, and I'm not really a writer. God had other plans though, and thankfully I wasn't stupid enough to ignore them. I felt like God was telling me I needed to start writing my own curriculum. Two years later, and I not only write curriculum for the kids in my own ministry, I am now a curriculum provider. I share all of this because I believe that God has new gifts He will give to you in every new season if you are open to receive what He has for you.

Still not sold on the idea that you could be creative and just haven't realized it yet? Here's a great idea for you—pray for creativity! Why not? John 14:14 NLT says, "Yes, ask Me for anything in My name, and I will do it!" If you desire creativity to do what you know God has called you to do, ask for it. My professor and mentor in college, Dick Gruber, used to share stories of his early years. When he first started in kids ministry,

Spark

it basically didn't even really exist. There weren't children's ministry majors in college, classes you could take online, or even curriculum to use. He and his wife basically fell into running a kids ministry, and they had to create most of what they did with the kids from scratch. He told us that he was a terrible artist when he was younger, but he prayed, and God gave him the ability to draw and create coloring pages and salvation booklets for kids. He told us he didn't know how to act or play a musical instrument, but God gave him the ability to create his most famous character, Sam Saint, who plays the piano while he tells his stories. Now, I will admit that when Professor Gruber shared those things with us, I remember a voice of doubt in my mind that said to me, "That won't happen for you. You just aren't creative." I know I listened to that voice and believed it at the time, but I never forgot those stories. It gave me hope that God could use me in new areas if I was willing and ready.

Creativity can be elusive. You may find that your creativity is affected by your surroundings. You need to find your creative place. What gets your creative juices flowing? Do you work well alone? Or are you more creative with a team of people throwing out ideas? Do you need complete silence or constant noise? Does working from home make you more productive, or do you need to get out of the house to avoid distractions? A creative place is going to be different for everyone. I personally prefer working from home, by myself, and in complete silence. Because I know that is my consistent creative place, I have chosen to take one day every week to write and create curriculum at home.

Other times, when you find yourself hitting the creative wall, switching up your location can make all the difference. If working at home isn't working for me, I like to go to a quiet coffee shop. It's nice to get a little treat because I'm a huge coffee lover, but it also changes up my environment and provides new inspiration. Sometimes, I take it a step further and occasionally take weekend getaways to write and create for a

Help! I'm Not Creative

lengthy period of time without all of life's distractions. The incredible creativity and peace you can experience just by looking out your window can be enough to kick your imagination into high gear. If you are willing to switch things up, you will find your own creativity.

Before you can get your creative juices flowing, every project needs a jumping-off point or springboard. You may want to start with a biblical passage, a topic, or a theme. It depends on the project, but my favorite springboard is typically a theme. A great theme will get your brain thinking so quickly that you won't be able to write the ideas down fast enough. I recently decided on my theme for writing next year's Vacation Bible School (VBS), and ideas were coming to my brain for hours after that. I'm sure you can think of a time when you were planning a project and came up with a theme that inspired you to the core. When you find a theme, topic, or biblical passage that inspires you to that level, you know you've found the perfect springboard for your project.

I'm sure that as many of you are reading this book, at least some of you have a similar personality to mine—Type-A. People with a Type-A personality enjoy staying organized but can use that as an excuse as to why they aren't creative. Early on, I learned to embrace my Type-A creativity, because creativity is so much better with lists. This is where creativity meets organization, and they can be the best of friends. In my opinion, you can never have too many lists for a project. For example, I make lists to brainstorm ideas to make sure I don't forget anything. Lists can help keep the creative thinking process moving. When you keep all your ideas for a project crammed in your brain, it can drive you out of your mind. The ideas spiral around in your head, you worry about forgetting them, and you make mental lists over and over. Get out a pen and paper or your favorite note-taking software and start writing your ideas down! I've always been a huge fan of writing things down in a notebook, but sometimes notebooks get lost or left in one

Spark

place when you need them in another. I have recently shifted to using an electronic notebook for all my lists, and I will never go back. I have all my lists in one place, and they sync between my devices seamlessly, which means I have access to all my lists no matter where I am.

The creative process is not over once the planning is complete. It continues into the execution stage of the project. As you execute, you will tweak your ideas to make them fit the allotted time as well as cater them toward your specific audience. There's a fine line between boxing yourself into your plan and throwing it out completely. Allow yourself space to be creative and make it your own, and remember that it's ok to make changes that deviate from the original plan.

Most likely, you will never be the best at everything in your ministry, and that's ok. It's exhausting trying to do everything by yourself. Surround yourself with a team of creative people who have all the giftings you need to make ministry excellent. Find people who are great at drawing/painting, stage design, speaking, acting, writing, creating games/object lessons, technology, lighting, singing, and playing instruments. The list could go on forever. There are so many gifts that can be useful in the kids ministry. Find people of all ages, from different walks of life, and from every vocation, and ask them what they would do to make your ministry even better. We are always more effective when we partner with a group of people with different perspectives than ours. Let's find them and work together to reach kids creatively and effectively.

CREATIVITY CHALLENGE

Try something new this week. You could find an ambitious recipe to cook, make something you pinned on Pinterest, or teach yourself how to juggle. You never know what you will be good at and love doing until you give it a try. Spend five minutes every day asking God to reveal new areas of creativity He is wanting to grow in you.

chapter 3

INVITING ENVIRONMENTS

OVER THE LAST FEW YEARS, I can't emphasize the importance of having inviting environments enough. Our environments often play a big role in the first impression families have when they walk into our ministries. They may have already formed negative or positive feelings about our kids ministry before they speak to anyone simply based on the feeling and appearance of our environments. Studies and surveys have shown that many people determine whether or not they will return to a church within their first five minutes on the premises. Think about that for a moment. That means that most people have already decided if they are going to have a closed or open mind to our churches before they have experienced our services. Our environments may not be the only thing that makes or breaks the experience for families in those first five minutes, but it is certainly going to be one of the more important factors. People may not even realize it, but environments really do matter.

Think about the different businesses you frequent. Many people choose not to go back to a doctor's office based on the waiting room and patient rooms alone. People will choose to

Spark

pay more money for smaller cups of coffee because of a trendy and comfortable vibe in a coffee shop. I know this whole subject of environments may even seem shallow, but we would never neglect other aspects of first impressions in our churches. The lobby, greeters, check-in experience, and even the coffee shop are of utmost importance, and our kids ministry environments are speaking to the families who enter our churches, whether we like it or not.

I didn't always understand the importance of environments. I had always seen kids ministries where the environments looked the same for years, even decades, and it just seemed normal. I thought you needed a big budget to hire an outside company to do a total overhaul on your environments, and then you could just call it good to go. When I went into my first ministry position, I faced the challenge of sharing most of my ministry environments with other ministries in the church on top of having a tiny budget. I thought there wasn't a lot I could do to make our environments look exciting and inviting when I had to set everything up and tear everything down each week. I have since learned that the only true limitation to what you can do with your environments is your own creativity. There is nothing you can't do with a little ingenuity and creativity, and it will always be worth the extra effort in the end.

Who exactly are we aiming at inviting into our environments? At first glance, the answer may appear to be the obvious—kids. However, anyone who has been doing kids ministry for a few years knows that it's not just about the kids, but let's start there. What are kids looking for in an environment they are entering for the first time? There are two main things: familiarity and fun! I don't think very many people love going to a place for the first time. It can be scary, intimidating, and lonely. Kids want to feel at home in your ministry, or at least feel like they are experiencing something familiar to them. Kids also love having fun. Obviously, church shouldn't be all

Inviting Environments

about fun and no substance, but the fun is how we draw them in to hear the substance, which is the Gospel in our case.

How do we accomplish that? We use fun lighting, familiar music, and a game area to draw the kids in initially. There is something for everyone to help them feel comfortable and forget about those nervous first-time jitters. We never keep our environments looking the same for long. We want kids to be anxious to come back to our ministry and see what's new! Kids in your ministry will be so excited when they walk into a new and fresh environment that they will actually want to invite their friends to church. It keeps them guessing and on the edge of their seats to find out what the next theme will be and to see what all the new decorations are.

Let's talk about another audience we should definitely be trying to reach: the parents. This audience is a little bit harder to impress, but we don't want to miss out on impacting them. After all, kids cannot drive themselves to church, so if you don't have parental approval and support, you probably won't get very far reaching their kids. Other than our volunteer team, our environments may be the only first impression we are able to make on parents. Most parents will never attend one of your kids services, but they will experience your check-in area, hallways, and rooms. I love seeing the surprised looks on the parents' faces when they see our ministry environments for the first time. You can tell that it wasn't what they were expecting, but in a good way. It's good to keep them guessing.

My favorite compliment I ever received was from a parent during one of our series that was loosely based on the Indiana Jones movies. The parent told me that our main kids' room reminded them of Disneyland. You can't beat that, especially when you spent almost nothing on all of the environment décor and found most of it in the attic. I love choosing themes and creating set pieces that the kids think are fun but excites the parents too. The energy and time we spend making our environments look exciting and inviting speaks volumes to parents about our ministry. They see the passion and hard work that goes into our environments, and it lets them know we really care about executing a quality kids ministry in other areas as well.

The last audience may not be as important as the first two, but it's definitely worth mentioning—your volunteer team. I've found that people love being a part of something new and exciting. When we create inviting environments for kids and parents, we are creating a ministry that our volunteer team can be proud of. We want our volunteers to be excited to be part of a thriving ministry and want to invite their friends and family to serve alongside them. My volunteers often tell me that they wish they had a kids ministry like ours when they were young.

One way to target your volunteers' interest is to provide an inviting environment for them as well. Maybe you have the space to have an entire room devoted to your volunteers, or maybe you just have the space to give them a little corner. It goes a long way to show your volunteers that you care about them and appreciate them. In our case, we set aside a small area backstage in our main kids ministry room just for our volunteers. We provide breakfast food, snacks, drinks, a place to put purses/personal belongings, and anything else the volunteers might need. We want to make it easy and comfortable for people to be a part of our team. When the volunteers are happy to be there, they are more welcoming to parents, and it rubs off on all the kids as well.

It is so important to keep your environments up to date, and I believe that a big part of creating an inviting environment for kids and families is changing it on a regular basis. I know it doesn't sound simple or even easy depending on your situation. It would be a whole lot easier to have a great theme and stick with it, but it wouldn't be the most effective way to create an inviting ministry for kids, parents, and volunteers. You can have the coolest kids ministry environments in the world in 2018, but in 2019, it won't be so fresh. Technology,

Inviting Environments

trends, and even the kids we are ministering to are constantly changing, and our environments should be no exception.

That brings us to a very important question: How often should we change our environments? The answer is going to look different for every ministry and will vary depending on the season your ministry and your church is in. I try to change up my base environments one or two times a year. That means re-organizing, giving things away, checking the paint on the walls, re-formatting the set-up of rooms, and deep cleaning. A good rule of thumb is to walk through your ministry environments as if you were a first-time guest. What do you see, smell, hear, and touch? Sometimes we don't notice the clutter or smells in our spaces because we are in them all the time.

In addition, I like to do temporary, theme-related set designs in our kids ministry to keep things new and exciting. We change our themed set design in our upper elementary and lower elementary rooms to go along with every new curriculum series we use. I have learned that changing the set design every month can become a bit much, so my favorite length of series is about 6-8 weeks. It evens out to be a new set design every other month or between six and eight times a year. It's a lot more doable for you and your team, and easier on the budget as well.

CREATIVITY CHALLENGE

Walk into each of your kids ministry environments and imagine seeing them for the first time through the eyes of a family that's never been to your church. Make a list of things you see that make your environments feel inviting. Make another list of things that could possibly make them feel uncomfortable. Don't forget to look at the small things too. Details matter in creating excellent environments that make families want to return to your ministry.

chapter 4

GIVING YOUR ENVIRONMENTS A FRESH LOOK

ONE OF MY FAVORITE THINGS to do in kids ministry is to cultivate awesome environments that make kids want to come back to church and invite their friends to come with them. When I first came to my third ministry position, one of the first things they asked me to do was give the kids ministry environment a fresh look. Our hallway and kids ministry rooms had looked the same for ten years, so it was time for something new. Whether you are new in a position or have been in your position for a while, ask yourself this question: "When was the last time you changed something about your kids ministry environment?" If it has been more than a couple of months, chances are you may need a change to give your environment a new feel.

Spark

I want to share five key steps we have taken in our kids ministry environments to give them a fresh look. Good news for those of you who are on a tight budget, most of these steps won't cost you a lot of money, if any.

Step 1: Declutter and Dispose

This step won't cost you any money, but it will require some hard work and elbow grease to get the job done. Go into each of your kids ministry rooms, hallways, check-in areas, storage closets, etc. and look around. More than likely, there are some items that need to go in the dumpster, or at the very least need to be relocated. Get rid of those items that you were saving for who-knows-what and make room for some nice, new options. We used to have an old air hockey table in the back of our main kids' room. It didn't even work and had become a dumping ground for all kinds of random stuff. Needless to say, we got rid of that and it made a huge difference. We started with our check-in area and upper elementary room, and it was amazing to hear parents, leaders, and even children noticing the change. Invite your team to come out and help you with this step. Some of your leaders might even know what needs to go better than you do!

Step 2: Organize and Label

The next step is to organize and label everything that is left after the purge. It's great to get rid of the clutter, but if you don't get it all organized and labeled, the clutter comes back in no time. We go through our storage areas one or two times a year to keep it organized and manageable. If you don't have enough storage after you have gone through everything and gotten rid of what you don't need, you might want to consider adding more storage. You may not have an extra closet just waiting to be filled, but you could create some using pipes and drapes and shelving. We used them to create two storage areas in our upper elementary room that also doubles as a backstage area and leader area for our team. When you are finished, everything should have a place and clear label. All your leaders should be able to find what they're looking for and put it back in its place when they are done with it. Don't get lazy and skip this step. It will save you lots of time and money when you can quickly locate the materials you need for your ministry.

Step 3: Paint the walls

This step may not apply to your ministry if it has been painted in the last year or two, but otherwise, your walls could probably at least use a touch up. You can simply repaint your walls in the same colors or go for a totally new look. Paint is cheap and if you want to change it again in a year or two, it's easy to do so. If your kids ministry has a logo or branding, you can tie your branding into your environments by using the same colors. I prefer to paint my elementary rooms a nice neutral gray, so I can switch up my temporary set designs and not clash with bright colors on the wall. In early childhood classrooms, I would choose one wall as an accent wall that is painted a fun color and decorated with some shape. I would leave the other three walls a neutral color.

Step 4: Switch it up

You may be able to give your environment a fresh look by simply switching things around in some of your rooms. Our upper elementary room has a lot of layout options. When we first inherited the room, there was a small permanent stage in one of the corners. While there wasn't anything wrong with the stage or its location, we wanted to move the stage to the center of the longest wall in our room. We couldn't salvage the corner stage, so we demolished it and installed some stage pieces that we already had at the church. Look around your church in storage areas for items that are no longer being used. We found lighting, trussing, stage pieces, and decorations that didn't cost us a thing to use but helped give us a fresh look. What may be old junk to one ministry could be new and fresh for yours. The area that used to be our stage was turned into extra storage and a leader hangout space using pipes and drapes. In a three-year period, we have moved our entire room and stage around three times. The last time we switched things up, we didn't even spend a lot of money. We mostly used things we had on hand, but we moved things around enough that it gave the impression that we had gotten a new screen, stage, and lighting.

Step 5: Get a Wow Factor

This step can be costly depending on what your wow factor is. We decided to put in a new screen as our big wow factor when we did our first big room move. It only cost us about $300, but people are still talking about it three years later. A wow factor for you might be new lighting, some large decorations on the walls, a new screen or LED wall, new signage, or anything else that will be obvious to families and kids when they enter your environment. More recently, we added some small framed "screens" around the room we made from insulation foam and mounted some projectors to create environmental projection all over our room as another wow factor. We can change the images to go along with different series at the click of a button, and it doesn't cost us anything. A wow factor might be something that costs you a larger investment in the beginning, but it should be something you can use and re-use for years to come.

Remember, your environment is a huge part of your first and final impression on kids and families when they walk into your church. When your environment is clean, well-painted, and fun, it shows families how much you care about excellence in your ministry. Even if you only do one or a couple of these steps at first, it will give your environment a fresh look that people are sure to notice.

ENVIRONMENTS DO'S AND DON'TS

I have grown to love creating set designs in our kids ministry environments over the last few years. I have many wonderful memories from set design days, and there is nothing like seeing the kids' faces light up when they walk into a room with a fresh design. However, along with the many great memories, there have been a lot of learning experiences. Some set designs turned out amazing, while others required a lot of upkeep and repair. I've definitely learned some things the hard way through trial and error, so I'm hoping to save others from my early pitfalls and missteps. Here are my top environments do's and don'ts.

1. Do use lots of tape to hang décor.

I learned the hard way that a little bit of tape doesn't go a long way. This is especially true if you are hoping to keep your set design up for more than a week. Put the amount of tape you think is enough, then add 50% more. Trust me on this, tape is not the place to cut corners.

2. Don't use the wrong tape for the job.

All flavors of tape are not created equal. There's a reason there are so many different types of tape out there. Tape can range from not being strong enough to hold décor to taking paint off the walls. Here is a list of my favorite tapes to use for various purposes and whether it is wall safe:

Gorilla Tape – A shiny black tape you can find at Walmart or any hardware store. It can be used for taping décor semi-permanently to surfaces that are not painted. I use this tape for taping up décor on pipe and drape, trussing, and staging. This tape will take paint off the wall.

Gaff Tape – A dull black fabric tape you will have to purchase online or at a music/pro audio store. I buy my gaff tape on Amazon. It is pricey, but worth it. It can be used for taping electrical cords to the floor and walls and taping décor on fabric or carpeted surfaces. Gaff tape doesn't leave a residue on anything like gorilla tape or duct tape does. It normally is safe for painted surfaces except in cases of extreme heat (over 100° F).

Double-sided Duct Tape – A light blue roll of tape, usually found at Walmart. It can be used for taping décor together. I mainly use this tape when I'm too lazy to pull out the hot glue gun. I use it to turn one-sided décor into double-sided décor, or to tape paper décor to cardboard to make it sturdier. It's a real lifesaver when you're in a pinch. It takes paint off the walls.

Mavalus Tape – A white or cream roll of tape. You can purchase it at tcacher stores, but I believe it is cheaper to purchase from Amazon. It can be used for taping lighter décor to walls or ceilings, and it doesn't take paint off the wall. My only complaint is that they need to start selling this tape in bigger rolls!

3. Do hang décor from the ceiling.

It might seem like a lot of extra work, especially if your ceilings are high enough to need a large ladder, but it's worth it. Hanging décor from the ceiling takes your design from a two-dimensional stage to the entire environment.

4. Don't make your ceiling décor one-sided.

There are lots of awesome decorative signs you can buy or create to fit your theme. Don't make the mistake of hanging your décor, then realizing that you can only see it if you happen to be standing in the right place. Take the time to make your décor double-sided, so no matter where a person is standing or sitting, they will see it.

5. Do use clear fishing line for hanging décor.

Fishing line is a wonderful tool to have in your set design tool box. It is nearly invisible and extremely cheap. You can buy a giant roll of clear fishing line at Walmart for about $3. It is perfect for hanging light décor like signs or paper lanterns from the ceiling.

6. Don't forget to triple knot your fishing line.

I learned early on that when you knot fishing line once, it comes undone. This is particularly annoying if you used it to hang decorations from the ceiling using a tall ladder, and you come in on a Sunday morning to find everything lying on the floor. I have learned to triple-knot fishing line every time. It is worth the extra effort to not have to pull out the giant ladder again.

7. Don't be afraid to use paint.

I used to be hesitant to use paint because it seemed so permanent, but paint really isn't that expensive, and items can always be re-painted later. When we did a big overhaul on our upper elementary room, we bought some stage pieces that were in good condition but desperately needed a coat of paint. We saved hundreds of dollars by simply being willing to re-paint them.

8. Do make sure you use the right tools.

Before you start your painting project, make sure you have everything you need to get the job done correctly and avoid a large mess. You will need lots of drop cloths, gloves, paint brushes, painter's tape, and clothes you don't mind getting ruined. If you are going to be inside, make sure you have proper ventilation. If you are painting outside, don't just assume the rain will wash away the paint. I spray-painted some cardboard rockets on the church lawn once, and we had silver rocket silhouettes on the lawn for weeks. That's not a fun conversation to have with your Lead Pastor on a Sunday morning.

9. Don't get stuck on your curriculum.

Curriculum is an incredible tool that many of us have the privilege of using. It's a great place to start, but don't be afraid to go off curriculum every once in a while. You don't have to write your own curriculum all the time, but if you get an idea that

Spark

doesn't line up with where the curriculum is going, don't ignore your idea!

10. Do pay attention to culture.

The kids in our ministries are immersed in an ever-changing culture each day. Do you know what movies and TV shows your kids are watching? What bands or artists are they listening to? What toys or video games are on their Christmas list? If you know the answers to these questions, it will help you create environments and themes your kids will love. Sometimes, your curriculum will do this for you, but other times the curriculum can be way off. Don't depend on your curriculum to tell you what your kids are excited about right now.

I hope this list of do's and don'ts made you laugh, and will help you avoid some of the failures I have experienced in the world of environments.

Creativity Challenge

Take a fresh look at your environments and begin taking the first couple steps in giving your environments a clean and fresh look. Your regularly-attending families may have gotten used to the pile of junk that is sitting in the corner of the room, the chipped paint on the walls, and the dust gathering on every surface, but even they will notice when you give your environments a much-needed facelift.

_____
_____
_____
_____
_____
_____
_____
_____
_____
_____
_____
_____
_____
_____
_____
_____
_____
_____
_____

chapter 5

ENVIRONMENTS ON A BUDGET

IN THIS CHAPTER, I want to focus on the idea of changing up your environments on a regular basis. Temporary set designs may already be a part of your ministry because your curriculum might provide great theming ideas to accompany each series. If temporary set designs have never been a part of your ministry, you might be hesitant about adding this option to your already-full kids ministry plate. I totally understand how you might feel that way, but I believe a fun set design change every six to eight weeks can make a huge impact on the excitement and engagement of kids and families in your ministry. If you've never given set design a try, you may buy into one of three most common myths explaining why you can't do set designs in your ministry.

Myth #1 – Space

At this point in ministry, I am blessed with my own elementary kids ministry environment. However, many kids ministries have to share their environment. Whether that's with other ministries in the church, a school, or other groups that meet in their ministry spaces during the week, it can be a challenge to decorate in those shared spaces because everything has to be portable to facilitate set-up and tear-down each week. Some churches may be in a situation where they don't own the building they meet in each weekend. That situation is particularly challenging because everything must be set-up and torn down each week, including screens, chairs, and sound systems. This may make it more challenging to theme out your environment, but it shouldn't stop you from doing it. If something is important and worth doing, there are ways to make it happen!

For example, in our lower elementary breakout room, we keep our set-up simple. We have a couple of orange rugs we bring into the room for seating, a rolling cart that contains the message and game supplies for the week, and we create a couple lightweight set pieces to go along with the current series. Most items are constructed with cardboard, insulation foam, boxes, and occasionally inflatables. The goal is to keep everything light and easy to carry. We also have a TV in the room that we use to add theming for each series. Since every situation is different, I talked with several other kids pastors who are changing up their environment every month despite being portable. It's impressive and totally doable. Here are some suggestions they mentioned.

- Have a themed table outside your ministry areas for parents and families to visit. This allows them to see what the kids are learning about each week. Your themed table might include your current curriculum series theme, the series verse in a picture frame, props to go along with the series, fun little toys or candies as incentives, and information about upcoming events in the kids ministry.
- You can print posters of the series theme and verse, frame them with a cheap frame from IKEA, and place them on easels. If you or someone on your team is artistic, you

Environments on a Budget

could even buy a large whiteboard or chalkboard you can decorate to go along with the theme for each series.

- For your stage, you can use pallet walls on wheels as backdrops that are easily changeable and can be stored in a trailer.
- Keep all your supplies lightweight and/or add wheels to them so they are easy to move in and out.

The one thing all of these ideas have in common is they are simple, and anyone can put them into action. If you are in a difficult space situation in your current ministry, choose one or two of the ideas above and make it your own. Set design doesn't have to be extravagant to make a big impact on your ministry.

Myth #2 – Creativity

We have already discussed this myth quite a bit in Chapter 2, but here is your reminder. Don't let a lack of personal creativity in the area of set design keep you from trying this out in your ministry. Don't count yourself out because you think you aren't creative or artistic. If set design just isn't your thing and you have no interest in learning how to do it, there are probably people in your church who would love to do it. Seek out people for your set design team who love building things, crafting, sewing, drawing, painting, or who just think it sounds like fun, and start delegating. I've spent several years doing a lot of my set designs alone or with one other person, and I finally found someone who loves doing set designs even more than I do! As a bonus, she is an amazing artist who can draw and create things I never could have dreamed of creating myself. She loves taking things home to work on and even uses her own art supplies most of the time. She thanks me for giving her an outlet to use her artistic abilities. There is nothing better than finding someone who helps you fill a need in your ministry and thanks you for allowing them to be a part of it. That's a win for everyone involved. You never know who is out there in your

Spark

church just waiting to be asked to use their creative talents in your ministry. It never hurts to ask!

Myth #3 – Budget

I hear a lot of talk about budget being an issue or hindrance for many kids ministry leaders. This is one of the top two common struggles most kids pastors have in their ministries. It's right up there with not having enough volunteers. Most kids pastors would agree that they don't have a big enough budget to do all the things they want to do, and some don't even have a budget at all. If that is the case, you shouldn't let that stand in the way of changing up the environment. It will just take a little more creativity and imagination to get the job done. I have created many set designs that didn't cost me a cent just by using items already on hand or items that could be found for free. I've discovered that when I have a big budget, I tend to just go out and buy things, but when I have a smaller budget or no budget at all, I have more creative ideas because I am forced out of my comfort zone to find a solution. A good place to start is with the three Rs: re-use, repurpose, and recirculate.

Re-use: What items do you already have on hand from a previous event or set design that you could use again without changing anything? When you are tearing down after an event or set design, make sure you save any items that you could potentially use again by putting them in a storage container and labeling them clearly, so you can find them again when you need them. Go dig through those storage closets in your church and find some hidden treasures that you can re-use. Don't limit yourself to items you can find in your own department. Talk to the Youth Pastor, Worship Pastor, or Women's Ministry Pastor and ask if they would allow you to borrow items from their departments. Most of the time, other ministries are happy to share their resources with you. Just make sure you are extra careful with items you borrow and always put them back

Environments on a Budget

the way you found them. This will help you maintain a healthy and positive relationship with other ministry departments.

Repurpose: What items do you already have on hand or lying around that you could modify and turn into something fresh and new? That's what I have done with spare wood pieces, sheets of cardboard or poster board, trash in the church, kraft paper, and old decorations. If you made a sign or decoration for one set, you might be able to turn it around and use the other side for something else. You might be able to cut a piece of foam board or cardboard into a new shape and paint over the old paint. Don't throw it away until you have thought about how it could be repurposed for something new. Keep in mind that at some point, you may have to decide to part ways with something if you haven't used it in a year or two. You need to be able to walk into your storage areas and actually find the items you need without wading through piles of junk.

Recirculate: What items could you possibly borrow or have donated by someone in your church or community? Just because you don't already own the item or you don't have the budget to buy it doesn't mean there's not someone in your church or community who does. What items do you have on hand that you could donate or loan out as a resource to other ministries? I have been on the giving and receiving end of this, and it has been such a blessing to my ministry and to other ministries. If throwing out set pieces you worked tirelessly on is breaking your heart, it can make you feel a lot better knowing you are able to bless someone else with the chance to use it.

A couple of years ago, we created countless homemade decorations for VBS. Knowing that we were going to have to tear most of our creations down and throw them in the trash after only four nights was quite disheartening. On the third night of VBS, I had a group of parents who I didn't even know approach me about taking the decorations after VBS was over. They just happened to be on the decorating committee for a similar-themed event that was happening at a local public school in the fall. This was truly a God-moment for both of us! They were thrilled to receive all our decorations for free, and they offered to bring a team of people to come tear all the decorations down on the last night of VBS. It was so cool knowing that our VBS decorations, which had been prayed over and hung on the walls and ceilings of our church, were going to be re-used in a public school setting. Always be willing to help others and God will bless you in return.

When creating the temporary set designs in your environments, always remember to think outside the stage. Think about your environment—it's more than just a stage. In fact, you may not even have a stage. Everyone's environments are going to look different. You may have one large room, multiple small classrooms, an entryway, an information table, a check-in area, hallways, etc. We have tried to make our environment a very simple blank slate. Our stage is portable, and the pieces are movable to allow for different stage set ups. We have large pieces of aluminum truss that can be moved around to create different looks, a large center screen, and lighting to create a different feel for each series. We can accomplish a lot of theming in our environment just by using technology. Whenever possible, bring your theme out into your entire environment. Don't just decorate the front of the room or the stage. Decorate the walls, the entryway, and the ceiling. Find ways to extend your theming out to the entrance or check-in areas. This ensures that adults and parents see that you are doing something awesome and different in your kids ministry, and it will draw them in to check out your environments even further.

If you keep the budget-friendly items below on hand, you will be able to create most temporary set designs.

1. Tape—We use tape a lot in set designs, especially in our less-permanent sets. It takes a lot of trial and error to find out which type of tape works best for what application, which tape doesn't take the paint off the walls, and how much tape to use.

Environments on a Budget

2. Fishing Line – While it may seem like an odd item to be on this list, if you haven't used fishing line before, you are going to love it. It is super cheap to buy, and you get a roll big enough to last you at least a year. I use it for hanging decorations from the ceiling or trussing. Since fishing line is clear, it makes decorations look like they are almost floating in midair. You can also use it to attach heavier props and decorations to banners, stage pieces, and trussing without it being visible from a distance.

3. X-acto Knives/Mixed Media Scissors—X-acto knives are great for cutting just about anything. You don't have to plug them in, they just require some elbow grease. They are particularly great for cutting through cardboard, but you can also use them for cutting through thin foam board (not the thick insulation foam). I have a lot more luck with getting the precision I want when using an x-acto knife on cardboard. I will usually trace or draw my shape(s) in pencil, then cut the cardboard with the x-acto knife. Mixed media scissors are another must-have for cutting out circles or difficult shapes out of cardboard—they're just not as good at detail work as x-acto knives.

4. Foam Board/Poster Board—I use both for making large signs/decorations to either hang from the ceiling or attach to the stage or trussing. You can make a hanging foam board decoration double-sided by gluing colored poster board to the back side of it and cutting out the same shape. You can also use poster board sheets to decorate large cardboard stand-up decorations as well.

5. Cardboard Sheets/Boxes—I have a serious love of large sheets of cardboard. That may sound ridiculous, but when I look at a fresh, blank sheet of cardboard, the options are endless. I can make any shape, decoration, cut-out, or prop out of that free sheet of cardboard. Just cut it up with an x-acto knife, slap on some paint, poster board, or glitter, and you are good to go. Cardboard boxes can be used for props by painting them or covering them in kraft paper. Cardboard may look boring, but the creative possibilities are endless.

6. Cardstock/Craft Foam Sheets – If you just need a colored shape, go for craft foam. If you need a printed image, use cardstock. If you buy the big 12×18 sheets of craft foam, you can make bigger decorations that feel more 3D as opposed to paper or cardstock creations.

7. Hot Glue/Hot Glue Gun—I don't know about you, but I can be a bit impatient when I am putting together set designs, especially when I'm under a time crunch. That's why hot glue is my favorite type of glue for just about anything. Hot glue does require you to be careful to not burn yourself, but it dries so quickly that it's worth the risk. I use hot glue to glue together large cardboard props and signs. I don't recommend using it on wood, but it's excellent to use on paper, foam, and cardboard.

8. Spray Paint/Craft Paint—Spray paint is great for getting a nice base color on large cardboard props. Painter's tape and stencils can also be used to tape off different parts of the cardboard to make shapes and designs out of the unpainted sections. I use small bottles of acrylic craft paint for painting more detailed designs or words on props. Spray paint will disintegrate most foam, so stick to acrylic paint or house paint for foam items.

9. Kraft Paper Rolls—I am talking about the huge rolls of kraft paper that you can buy on Amazon, not those tiny, expensive rolls of bulletin board paper they sell at teacher's stores. I have almost every color kraft paper that is available from various projects, and the options are seemingly endless. Whether it's blacking out windows for a blacklight set, covering tables, walls, boxes, or the entire stage, or making fake vines and treasure maps, its versatility is truly amazing.

10. Pinterest—While I do come up with some great ideas without it, I can say that I have gotten a lot of amazing ideas

Environments on a Budget

from searching on Pinterest. There is no need to reinvent the wheel. I always check on Pinterest to see if anyone has already done something similar and written a tutorial before I try to make it up the hard way on my own. Sometimes, just looking at other people's ideas sparks a new idea that is just what I need for my project. I like to create unique boards for each of my set designs, so I can easily go and look at the pins I pinned for that particular set.

This is by no means a comprehensive list of items I use in my set designs, but it is definitely a great place to begin if you are just getting started in set design. These are all items I keep on hand, and I use at least half of these items in every set design I do.

Creativity Challenge

Make a temporary set design budget for an upcoming curriculum series or event. It could be $0, $50, or even $100. Create a set design plan and execute the plan. Try to stay under budget. If this is your first set design, keep it simple. You may surprise yourself with what you can create with little to no budget.

chapter 6

STRATEGIC EVENTS

Events are a big part of what we do in kids ministry and can take up to 50% of our time depending on the time of the year. You may as well add the title *Event Coordinator* to the endless list of responsibilities you will be expected to fulfill unless your church is large enough to hire someone who handles all the events. The fact that some churches have full-time event coordinators tells you something about how much time events can take to plan, organize, and execute. However, many of us may have never thought about why we do the events we do in our churches. We just keep doing them year after year. Successful events require a lot of creativity and strategy to be done well.

In my first ministry position, I primarily did events that had always been done in that church. I executed events that I had seen done before at other churches and just assumed that those were the events I should do in my ministry as well. I don't even remember thinking about why we did those events in the first place or if they were actually effective.

During my second ministry position, it became clear very early on that we were an event-driven church. If I didn't have some kind of kids ministry event on the calendar every other week, I wasn't doing enough events. I once made the mistake of saying we weren't planning to do any events for the month of August because we had done five events in July and our team needed a little break. My Lead Pastor's response was that we needed to make every Sunday in August and September a big Sunday and create an event for every week. The motivation for events was to get people through the door in the seats. This strategy didn't turn out to be very effective in the long run because families came to expect frequent events, so they didn't feel obligated to attend each one. They stopped caring about the events altogether, regardless of how awesome they were, because events had become like white noise to them. They were no longer special or exciting because they happened all the time.

Many churches fall into one of several event traps. Either they produce events for the wrong reasons, or they produce events for no reason at all. It's critical to be intentional and strategic about planning events. Many churches do events because "they've always done that way." That phrase gets thrown around countless times when discussing changing anything in a church. Just because we've always done it doesn't mean we should keep on doing it forever.

Sometimes, churches are cautious about changing events because they fear one or two prominent families will be upset if it doesn't happen. How often do we allow one or two people's opinions to dictate what we do because we are afraid of upsetting them or losing them from our church? If only a couple families are going to care about an event being cancelled, that's not a good reason to keep it around. Sometimes, we do the events because we personally love it and don't want to stop doing it. It might be a tough pill to swallow, but if the event is no longer effective or isn't a good fit for your church culture, it may be time to shut it down. Lastly, some events are produced "just for fun." I believe the biggest time-wasting event is the

Strategic Events

event we put on for no reason at all. Fun is great in ministry, but if that's the only reason an event happens, there is a better way you could be spending your time, energy, and resources. Remember, zero strategy often yields zero results.

When planning events, church leaders may ask: Why do we need to get strategic about the events we are offering? It would be so much easier to just keep doing things the way we have always done them. The answer is simple: If we truly believe that God has given us everything we have including our budgets, volunteers, positions, and time, it's our responsibility to find the best way to use those resources for Him. When we become intentional about creating an events strategy, we will begin to see results we have never seen before. Events shouldn't come and go without having an effect on your ministry or the families who attend them. An event can be the catalyst for families choosing to attend your church, for kids making true friendships with other kids their age who love God, and for people making the ultimate choice to accept salvation for the first time. You won't be able to accomplish all of these things in every event you plan, but you can think through each individual event and make sure it is accomplishing at least some of the goals you have.

The strategy for each event is different, so my strategy may look completely different from what the strategy for other churches needs to look like. There are a lot of factors that should be considered when you create your events strategy, and the first two questions to start with when determining event strategy are: "Who are you trying to reach?" and "What are you trying to accomplish?" These questions don't have easy answers, but they are a great place for you to start.

Talk with your leadership about who you are trying to reach first. The answer is affected by a number of factors, beginning with the area of the country or world you live in. Whether you live in a city or in a rural area, what people in your area value, and who other churches in the area are trying to reach. Then, look at your area demographics—the class and family size. The more you know about your audience, the easier it is to find ways to reach them.

Once you have your target audience, you need to know what you are trying to accomplish. This question needs to be asked for each individual event you plan. More than likely, each event will try to accomplish different goals with different types of events. Kids ministries often are in charge of kids-only events, family events, parent meetings and events, volunteer meetings and events, and community outreach events. Start by making a list of your goals for each type of event. This needs to be granular—a blanket list of goals for all the events you organize will not set you up for success.

As you begin to create a strategy for the events you plan, you may realize that some of the events you have been doing aren't fitting into your strategy. It is important to go into this process being willing to make some changes. Some of you may have gotten excited about the idea of making changes, while others may already be feeling stressed about rocking the boat or making someone upset. Change can be hard, but change is a good thing. You will need to update some of the events you are currently producing and possibly cut some altogether. If you want to try adding any new events to the calendar, you need to be willing to give up some of the old events. Don't make the mistake of piling new events on top of all of the old events you have always done. Not only is this a clear recipe for burnout for you and your team, but events are no longer special if they happen too frequently. Most people will get excited about the changes and will welcome new events to the calendar. Be ready to cast vision and give the strategy behind changing, eliminating, and adding new events. It always helps people understand change when you take the time to justify a reason behind it. Start with your Lead Pastor and once you've sold him on the changes, pitch it to your core team. If your Lead Pastor and your volunteer

Strategic Events

team are behind you making the changes, they will back you up if there are a few disgruntled families who disagree with your decisions.

As you create your strategy for events, keep your weekly service times in the forefront of your mind. Your main service times should always be your first priority. Never neglect your main service time with your kids because of a big event. It can be tempting to throw on a movie or have a party day in kids church when you have a major event coming up or you are experiencing the fatigue that comes with the aftermath of a huge event, but we must remember that part of our strategy for doing events in the first place includes wanting families to return to our churches on a regular basis. We don't want our normal kids services to be a huge letdown coming off an excellent event. We want our events to reflect what we do in our main kids services. Events needs to have a tie-in to your services, and should reflect a similar level of excellence on what is done on a regular basis. We shoot ourselves in the foot if we put all of our creative energy into making our events successful and leave nothing to spare for creating an above-average ministry experience during our main services. The kids deserve our best every week, not just for special events.

It's easy to get so caught up in planning our kids events and services that we begin to believe we are out on our own private island. Even though it may feel that way sometimes, it's not all about our kids ministry. If we plan events without considering this, it's only a matter of time before problems arise. There are a lot of factors outside our ministries that have a huge effect on how successful our events are. For example, it's probably not the best idea to plan your VBS on the same week as youth camp. You would lose the opportunity to use any of the students as leaders during the event. It's not a great idea to plan a kids event on the same weekend as another ministry's event. The families in your church have to prioritize what they attend in any given month, so don't make it a competition

Spark

between your ministry and other ministries in the church. The goal should always be to work together as a team to offer events and ministries that will complement each other. In addition, be aware of holidays. When kids in your area are on breaks from school, families tend to go out of town. Do your best to avoid planning events during those time periods, even if it means not being able to fit all of the events you had planned on the calendar. When we choose to ignore other ministries and outside events, we run the risk of making other ministries upset and having a low turnout for an event that would have otherwise been successful on a different date.

The culture in your church and community will play a big part in whether an event will be a huge success or a waste of your time. Ask yourself these questions. Do you know your church culture? What is important to the families in your church and community? Are the events you are currently offering meeting those needs and preferences? An event that may have been well attended in one area may not be a good fit for another. It is important to know your church and area culture, so you can make sure the events you are planning fit into it. Sit down with your Lead Pastor and ask him what his vision is for events? What does he really care about? If you don't know, it's time for you to have that conversation with him before you begin creating your strategy. Your Lead Pastor's vision for the church as a whole should always be the catalyst for everything we do in our ministries. His vision should be reflected in what your ministry is offering for events for the kids and families in your church and community.

It's almost time for you to begin creating a strategy of your own for the events in your kids ministry. Maybe you already have a strategy, even if it's just inside your head, and you need to become intentional about putting it down on paper or tweaking it to make sure you are considering all the important factors. I find it easier to create something of my own when I have someone else's plan as an example to start

Strategic Events

with, so here is my basic strategy for events that I follow. It is definitely not the best way or the only way to plan events, but it is what works for our current ministry and culture.

There are five different types of events we offer each year in the kids ministry department: kids-only, family, outreach, volunteer, and parent events. We offer at least one of each of the first three types of events (kids-only, family, and outreach) per quarter. Every event must have the Word of God and the Gospel message included. We don't do events just for fun or to fill time. All paid events (with the exception of camp) includes an option for guests to attend free of charge to encourage kids and families in the church to invite their friends who don't attend the church to come. All outreach events are free for everyone to attend. We have an events team staffed by volunteers and the kids pastors, and the team evaluates all major events at least twice a year. We use attendance numbers, interest level, and anonymous surveys to determine the effectiveness of events and if we will continue doing them in the future.

Creativity Challenge

Make a strategy for events in your ministry. Begin by making a list of what you believe is important to you, your church, and the community. Make a list of the events you are currently producing and see if they match up to the list of what is important. You can even talk to your Lead Pastor about what he is looking for and create a short anonymous survey for the families in your ministry to fill out. Consider changing or getting rid of events that don't meet your requirements, and brainstorm ideas for new events to replace them. This kind of change won't happen overnight, but you can begin making a shift in your ministry toward having a strategy for all of the events you plan in the future.

chapter 7
MAKE VBS GREAT AGAIN

VBS IS DEFINITELY NOT FOR EVERYONE. It may even be one of the events you are planning on cutting after making your strategy for events from Chapter 6. However, before you skip this chapter because VBS has been around for years, think about what you can do to make it more effective. If you are currently doing VBS every year in your church, there may be some small and large changes you can make to make this event fresh and attractive again. If you don't do VBS or you are doing something similar but aren't calling it VBS anymore, a lot of the ideas in this chapter will still be applicable to any large outreach events you are planning. Creativity isn't just about creating entirely new things, it's also about being able to make old things new again!

VBS is actually a relatively new event to me personally, even though it has been around for a long time in many churches. I produced my first VBS a few years ago, and I had no clue what I was getting myself into. I had only ever attended VBS when I was a little kid and had never even volunteered at a VBS or seen one in action as an adult. I heard a lot of the negative and positive arguments for and against VBS but had never taken on the event myself. I had my initial concerns, but I tried to go into my first VBS unbiased. I needed to be open to seeing if this event was right for me, our church, and our community, or if it was time to put it out to pasture. Honestly, I fell in love with VBS that first year and have become an advocate for continuing VBS in churches, after making some changes to make it relevant for the kids of today.

I want to address some of the primary arguments I have heard against doing VBS.

VBS is just too much work—This isn't necessarily incorrect, but it isn't exactly right either. If an event is effective, successful, and fits into your event strategy, it is worth extra work. VBS should be a lot of work if you are putting in the effort to make it an excellent event, just like any other large outreach event.

We just don't have the budget—This could be true, but budgets should never be a limiting factor in your ministry. There are always ways to stretch your budget for VBS or any other event.

VBS isn't effective anymore—Before you put it out to pasture completely, you may want to consider a few ways to adapt your VBS and change it up to make it effective for your kids ministry.

VBS requires too many volunteers, or I can't get enough volunteers—In my opinion, this can be a positive. An event that needs more volunteers than normal means you can get more of the church involved in the event. People who have never stepped foot in kids ministry will be immersed in it for the first time. VBS shouldn't be an event that is being put on by the kids ministry team alone. It should be an all-church, all-hands-on-deck community event.

You may need to cast that vision to your Lead Pastor so he can get behind you and ask the whole church to do their part. Remember, VBS is supposed to be an outreach event, so it

Make VBS Great Again

should not be aimed at church kids. If this is a problem at your VBS, there are some ways to get the word out to the community and ensure you reach more than just your regular church attendees.

Some may say VBS is overdone, but I would say that VBS is tried and true. Many people know what VBS is. It's a recognizable term even for unchurched families because it has been around for many years. Adults remember going to VBS when they were a kid, and they have fond memories of it even though they may no longer attend church anymore. VBS is great for the community if it's done the right way and for the right reasons. It doesn't matter if the kids that attend VBS attend another church, come to your church, or have never been to church in their lives.

Focus on the opportunity you and your church have to spend an entire week ministering to, loving on, and pouring into the kids of the community. It doesn't matter if parents think they are only bringing them because it's free babysitting for a couple hours. VBS is the best kind of babysitting I can think of! A lot of the emphasis on producing VBS can be placed on reaching the community, but VBS is great for the church as well. It is a great opportunity to get the people in your church excited about what the kids ministry is doing on a regular basis. It's your chance to gain visibility with church members who may never see what you do on a normal Sunday. Volunteers for VBS come out of the woodwork, and everyone can do their part and serve somewhere. My favorite thing about VBS is seeing my regular volunteers and new volunteers rally around one amazing goal: reaching kids with God's love.

If we are going to keep this classic event around, we need to find some ways to make it great again. It all starts with having a good plan in place. The first two things you need in your plan are a good theme and a detailed budget. Decide on your theme early, about a year out from the event if you can. Use a unique theme no one else will be using in your area. Take into

Spark

consideration what your kids are interested in and what your community loves to do. I would suggest picking a VBS theme that isn't brand new.

On the other hand, if you're feeling really daring, you can try your hand at writing your own. I used a packaged curriculum for my first VBS, but began writing my own the second time around because I wanted to personalize it. In this case, you need to get your budget together as early as possible. The earlier you submit the budget, the more likely it is to get approved. Even if your church doesn't require you to submit a budget for VBS, make one for yourself. Make your budget as detailed as possible and try to budget for everything. I like to work some things into the VBS budget that I can use throughout the year, like extra lighting, projectors, or hazers.

Putting together an events team is especially helpful for larger events like VBS. Your events team doesn't have to be limited to the people on your normal kids ministry team. Find people with a variety of talents: creative and artistic people for décor, technical people for the production, writers to help create content, foodies to help you put together the snacks, crafty people to help create hands-on activities, go-getters to advertise and ask for donations, people who love to cook, etc. The more variety you have on the team, the easier your events are to plan. Delegate different parts of the planning process of VBS to each person on the team. You have to start meeting early to do this effectively. I like to have my first events team meeting in November of the year before VBS and follow up with a couple more in the winter and spring.

Why so early? It's simple—your events team can help you with two other major components in the planning process: advertising and donations. We sometimes really miss the mark with advertising for large events. If no one knows our events exist, all our planning and hard work won't do any good. Good advertising options for the church include yard signs with event information, verbal announcements during services,

Make VBS Great Again

invite cards for families, and an information table in the lobby to allow people to learn more about VBS. To reach the community, we use large, full-color banners on the side of the road (facing both directions), Instagram/Facebook events with paid promotion, flyers in schools, guest contests, and using other events to promote VBS. The goal is to make sure VBS is placed on families' calendars before their summer vacation is planned to maximize attendance.

Once you have your dates in place, start looking for donations as early as possible. Donations can come from inside and outside the church. Ask a few members from your events team to start looking for donations early. They can submit donation requests online for many of the chain businesses and can talk with owners of local businesses in person. Many of the chains are willing to donate but must have more than a month's notice before your event. If family giveaways are part of your event, make it your goal to get all of the giveaways donated from outside the church. This can provide a huge cost savings and will allow you to put the donations/giveaways on promo cards to create more of a draw. In addition to business donations, create a donation list for in-house donations as well. Include snacks, crafts, games, and set design supplies on the list. It might help to create an online list or registry, so everyone can see what has already been donated.

The dates of your actual VBS aren't the only important dates you need to get on people's calendars. We offer training and information meetings for VBS as well as something we call Set Design and Pizza Nights, which are a time when people can come to the church and help create set design items for VBS. They typically last about three hours, and we eat lots of pizza. Kids are welcome, and we try to provide smaller jobs for them so they can feel like they're a part of making VBS happen.

We offer two trainings, two set design nights, opportunities for people to come to the church to help or take things home, and one big set-up day. Get these dates on the calendar early

Spark

and start promoting them at the beginning of the year. You can make a simple card you can hand out with all the important dates for VBS on it.

On the second training day, we break our leaders into groups based on the positions they will fill during VBS. This allows us to focus on specific training for each of the areas. There will always be people who want to help with VBS, but they never show up for any of the training sessions, so we create easy-to-use, straightforward leader packets for the majority of the volunteer positions. Each packet provides clear expectations and instructions for each leader in the front of the packet. I like to keep the expectations to one page and make it easy for people to know what they are doing even if they didn't make it to the meetings.

Environments are always important in kids ministry, but at VBS, they should be next-level. Don't be tempted to skimp on this because it's an easy area to cut costs. VBS may be the only time parents and other adults in the church see your kids ministry. They may never have a chance to see your services or small group rotations. We put between thirty and fifty percent of our VBS budget toward environments. That may seem like a lot, but between donations and reusing items we purchase for other events, it works out pretty evenly. Help your church leadership understand the importance of environments and cast vision to them first. Environments are what people talk about the most. Focus the majority of your energy and resources on common areas like the lobby, hallways, and main stage. Think about the areas the adults and parents will see the most. Come up with a wow factor for those common areas, something that will make people audibly impressed when they walk in. Clear signage is also important and can often be worked into the décor theme. If environments aren't your thing, make sure you have a couple people on your events team who excel in this area, so you can delegate to them.

The last and most forgotten part of the planning process is having a follow-up plan for families after the event is over.

Create this plan long before the event so it doesn't get forgotten in the post-VBS exhaustion phase. Decide who you want to follow up with and how you're going to do it. Get the information you need from families through registration cards or a giveaway. Calling or sending a postcard to 100 kids may sound daunting, but if you divide that up between all of the people on your events team, it becomes much more doable.

When planning VBS, keep these key points in mind.

Start early!

Start early on everything. I am always thinking about VBS somewhere in my brain. It's never too early to get started.

Get the word out!

Get the word out in every way possible to every person possible. Remember, the goal should be to get on families' calendars before their vacations are planned.

Aim older!

A great way to set yourself apart from other VBS-type events in the area may be to aim it at the older kids. Most VBS curriculums feel like they are aimed at younger children (K-2nd graders). I like to aim all of my ministry services and events at the oldest boys in the room. If they aren't engaged, you are likely going lose connection with the whole room. Think about what the older kids in your ministry like and incorporate it into every aspect of VBS.

Keep the focus on the Gospel!

Don't wait until the last night of VBS to talk about the salvation message. You might miss the opportunity to share Jesus with someone. Offer free Bibles for kids and families who don't own one. Don't be afraid to go a little deeper and challenge kids in the basics: prayer, the Word, sharing the Gospel with others, and living for God.

Make it relevant!

Ask yourself what is popular with the kids in your community. What is a theme that is going to draw kids and families into your church? What is going to make kids want to invite their friends? What is going to make kids want to come back to your church on Sundays? These are questions that will set you apart from the other events in the area.

Resemble your normal service options!

We shoot ourselves in the foot if our VBS is amazing and filled with live music, larger than life games, incredible environments, and special speakers, but our main service experience looks nothing like it. VBS is always going to be an above-and-beyond event, but we don't want families returning the following Sunday to be disappointed with the quality of our normal services.

Include the whole family!

You limit your influence by not involving the parents. We started offering a family night as the last night of our VBS and centered everything around the family. We review the week, play fun family games, give away family baskets, provide a challenge to the families, offer the salvation message, and have a VBS after-party. The after-party includes inflatables, balloon animals, face painting, food trucks, and an opportunity to hang out and connect with other families in the community. Advertise this well and include the giveaways and after-party options for the best attendance. You can also involve the family by sending home take-home cards each night to help parents engage with their kids once they get home. Another thing you can do is make the next Sunday a kid-themed service and invite everyone back to attend church as a family. This service gives you an opportunity to give testimonies from VBS and share what God has done with the entire church.

Make VBS Great Again

Don't be afraid to think outside the box!

You don't have to use the same VBS as every other church in town. Look at old VBS curriculum, find an obscure VBS no one else will be using, or write your own! Then, switch up your schedule/rotations and take a survey of the parents, kids, and volunteers to find out what they really love. The more unique your VBS is, the better your attendance will be.

Make your love for VBS contagious!

When you get the chance to share about VBS, don't just talk about the needs. Talk about your heart behind VBS. Why you love it, why it is important, and share testimonies from previous years. Let your passion and vision for VBS be evident when you speak to others, and they will catch it as well.

Creativity Challenge

Take some time this week to think about next year's VBS or another large event your ministry plans each year. Brainstorm some ways to change things up, think outside the box, and get more people excited about being part of it next year. Make a list of people you could invite to be a part of your events team and start reaching out to them now.

chapter 8

HOW TO CHOOSE THE BEST GAMES

GAME TIME SHOULD BE one of the most fun and creative parts of any great kids ministry. However, I know for a lot of ministry leaders, coming up with new and innovative games can be a struggle week after week. There is a lot of pressure in kids ministry to make sure our services are fun and keep kids coming back for more. We would love for parents to pick up their kids from kids church and ask them "What did you learn about the Bible today?", but the most common question they ask their kids is "Did you have fun?" Even though game time isn't the only thing that can be considered fun in our ministries, it is one of the first things we think of.

I will be the first one to admit that choosing games is not my favorite part of planning a kids service or event. Some kids ministry leaders can come up with ten games on the spot with no props needed. For other leaders, games may require more planning in advance. Games may not be the most important

Spark

element in a service or event, but they can make a huge difference in the impression we make on the kids during the brief time we have with them. I know many leaders who struggle with getting into a "game rut". They end up rotating the same three games until everyone is sick of them and they aren't fun anymore. Kids love simple games like Four Corners and Simon Says, but if those are the only games in your back pocket, the kids are going to get bored pretty quickly. I will address how I choose games for my ministry and different types of games for different occasions.

Before we get into the details on how to choose the best games, we need to ask the question: Why do we even need games in kids ministry? I have definitely asked myself this question more than a few times. I have even gone through seasons in my ministry where we would put the game at the end of the service and almost never end up playing it. The positive side of that mentality is that the kids still seemed to love coming to kids church and still had a fun time despite the absence of a game. It also made the kids really appreciate and love games when we brought them back to the middle of the service and began playing them again every week. While I may not believe games are always necessary, there are a few reasons they are useful in kids ministry and worth taking the time to incorporate into our services and events.

The first reason I would advocate for using games in your ministry is because kids all learn differently. Some of the kids who come into our ministries may learn the Bible story or the main point just fine while sitting still in their chair listening to the leader talk. Other kids will learn much better when they are out of their seat, playing an active game relating to the topic they're learning about. Games can be used as an alternative teaching method, and the kids won't even know they are learning something. It can be fun to use a teaching game in the middle of the message to draw the kids' attention back in or at the end of the message as an alternative to a traditional

How to Choose the Best Games

object lesson to drive the point home. Younger kids are going to have shorter attention spans and need to move around a lot more, so we break out our first and second grade kids for the last half of the service so they can have a shorter message time and more time for playing active games. Know your audience and use games to your advantage to keep the kids' attention and apply the message to their lives in a fun and creative way.

The second reason for playing games is a no-brainer: games are fun! Everyone can agree on the fact that games are fun to play and sometimes even more fun to watch. This seems pretty obvious, but if kids have fun when they come to church, they are more likely to want to come back the following week. I think adults might enjoy church more if there were games during their service too! That doesn't mean that we should use 20-30 minutes of service time playing games just for fun. There are always going to be exceptions to this rule. For example, when your service ends up going for two or more hours because a guest speaker doesn't know how to respect the service times. In those rare circumstances, by all means, play a few more games to keep the kids from going stir crazy. As a general rule, I shoot for spending 5-10 minutes on a game during a normal kids service time. Games are fun, but they are never worth taking the time you need for the message, worship, or small groups.

Games can help kids build new friendships and relationships, because they are relational by nature. They give kids the chance to get up out of their seats, talk with each other, and play together. Even if you are watching someone playing a game on a stage, you are connecting with them and relating to their desire to win. Most games require more than one person on each team, forcing kids to learn teamwork. When kids are chosen for games, they are thrown together with other kids they may not be friends with, and they quickly form a new bond with their new teammates through a shared goal of wanting to win the game. Games require kids to work together as a team and

Spark

interact with each other. Don't underestimate the ability of a five-minute game to help kids form new friendships.

Games can be such a broad category, and it's not like you are going to be able to use just any game for any occasion, so I like to break games up into five main categories.

Everyone Plays

These are games where everyone in the room gets a chance to play all at the same time. These types of games are the most popular with younger kids who get fussy and antsy watching other people play games. Younger kids all want to play all the time. Examples of everyone plays games would be Simon Says, Duck, Duck, Goose, Stand Up, Sit Down, or Human Rock Paper Scissors. There are lots of fun 'everyone plays' games to choose from and the best part is, they almost always require no extra supplies or set-up. This type of game can have the purpose of teaching something, or it can be played just for fun.

Stage Games

Stage games tend to be found in curriculum. These games only allow a few kids to play at a time, and everyone else gets to watch them playing the game. Stage games can be effective, but they can also fall flat and lose the attention of the audience. When done correctly, they can be entertaining and a lot of fun. The success of these games lies mostly with the person leading the game from the stage. If the leader is a lot of fun, knows how to get the kids hyped up, clearly explains the instructions of the game for everyone to hear, and keeps engaging the audience by having them cheer for the kids on the stage, these games can be a huge hit. Examples of stage games would be Minute to Win It style games, eating games, and review games. It is important to keep stage games short and snappy to keep the whole room engaged. Most stage games are just for fun, but some of them can tie into the message.

Outdoor Games

Outdoor games are probably not used on a regular basis during main services, but they can be a lot of fun at longer events or during mid-week services. Outdoor games usually fall under the 'everyone plays' type as well, but these are games you wouldn't dare to play inside because the kids might break something or there isn't enough room for them to run around. Examples of outdoor games would be capture the flag, anything involving a ball, and any variation of tag. Outdoor games usually have the purpose of getting the kids active and tend to take a longer amount of time.

Relay Races

I used to use a lot of relay races in my ministry, but I have found them to be less engaging than other types of games unless the group is small enough for everyone to play. Relay races require some or all of the kids to break up into teams, line up, and race to accomplish a goal one at a time. The problem with relay races is they can drag on for too long, and only a couple kids are fully engaged in the game at a time. My favorite way to use this type of game is to reiterate the verse we are learning in our series. You can put the words in the verse on any item, have the kids race to retrieve the items, then work together as a team to put the verse in order. The key to successful relay races is making it quick and easy for the teams to win.

Small Group Games

Small group games are a newer addition to the types of games we use in our ministry. I decided to give them a try to change things up because I felt like our stage games were falling a bit flat and the kids were getting bored with them. Our kids loved the small group games so much that we decided to start using them every week in our ministry. Kids of all ages love this type of game and they are the best at incorporating all of the best game elements. They are fall into the everyone plays category, they are relational, and it's easy to incorporate the message or the verse into the game. Small group games can be get-to-know-you games, verse games, or just for fun. Any game played in a small group is more personal and engaging for all of the kids involved. They may not be as flashy or look as fun as stage games, but the kids don't seem to care.

There are a lot of games out there to choose from, but all games are not created equal. I have used kids ministry curriculum that uses games all over the spectrum. Some have no games at all, while others just seem to throw random games into the curriculum for fun with absolutely no relevancy. It is a waste of everyone's time to play a game that has no point. When choosing or creating games for my ministry, I always ask myself three important questions.

Does it teach the point?

The point is whatever you want the kids to take away from the service when they leave. We call the point, "today's takeaway." For example, one of our takeaways about patience was "God's power gives us the strength to be patient." When I created the game, I wanted it to reinforce the idea of being patient. Right off the top of my head, I can think of at least three games that would teach this point and still be a lot of fun for the kids to play.

Does it fit the theme?

We always have a theme that accompanies our current curriculum series. When I am creating games to go along with the series, most of them are designed to fit into that theme.

Does it teach the verse?

One of my favorite ways to teach the verse to kids is through games. Verse games challenge the kids to memorize the verse so their team can win the game. You can fit a verse into almost any game, and you can write the verse on almost anything. My favorite item to use for verse games is balloons. You can put

How to Choose the Best Games

the verse on or inside the balloons, requiring the kids to pop the balloons to reveal the verse.

I don't require every game I choose or create to fulfill all three of these questions, but the game has to fulfill at least one and ideally two of the questions for me to use it at all. I believe that when we are intentional about choosing the games we use, they can be a great teaching tool, instead of just a time waster.

Creativity Challenge

Challenge yourself to get out of the "game rut." Take each of the five categories of games: Everyone plays, stage, outdoor, relay races, and small group games, and come up with one of each type of game. Remember to ask yourself those three questions: Does it teach the point? Does it fit the theme? Does it teach the verse? Make sure each game fulfills at least one of those questions.

chapter 9
OBJECT LESSONS OUT OF ANYTHING

OBJECT LESSONS ARE the most fun and creative way to teach a message in kids ministry. They are a combination of messages and creativity that drive the point home to the kids in our ministries. An object lesson or an illustration is any lesson that is taught using one or more objects or physical items. It is a practical example of a principle or idea. Often times, an object lesson will use items as symbols to signify a deeper or spiritual concept. Object lessons are particularly effective for older kids who have learned to cognitively grasp the idea of symbolism. That doesn't mean they can't be effective for younger kids as well, but they may require more of an explanation and need to be simplified to help them understand the meaning.

Jesus was one of the first people to use object lessons to teach people. He would often use items like a fig tree, a mustard seed, or some yeast to teach people spiritual truths. The parables of

Spark

Jesus were mostly object lessons, and Jesus used items that were culturally relevant to the people he was teaching to help them understand what he was saying. If Jesus thought object lessons were an effective way of reaching people with the Gospel, we should follow His example. Object lessons can also be a lot of fun, since they visually draw the audience in and grab their attention. You are more likely to retain information you learn visually and audibly. Visual learners will love object lessons because that is the way they will understand and process the message and remember what they learned in church that day.

Object lessons can and should be part of our services every week. Maybe that sounds like too often, or your curriculum doesn't include object lessons for you to use. You might be wondering how to come up with a new object lesson every week. It's quite simple if you don't overthink it. Object lessons are all about practical life applications, so find something that relates to the kids' everyday lives and create an object lesson around it. I like to use object lessons every week at the end of the message.

Our messages are broken up into three parts. We start with an introduction or a review on the topic for the day. Then, we follow up the review with a Bible story, and end with an object lesson and response time. Our object lesson is always the last thing we do before offering the kids an opportunity to respond after the message because we know the object lesson will get the kids' attention. It applies the message and God's Word to their lives, and draws them in to the response time. I want the kids to understand how the Bible story applies to their lives and drive the point home. I think if the main service would use object lessons more often, adults might remember more from the messages there, too.

Object lessons can be created out of anything. Many kids ministry leaders complain that their curriculum requires too many specialty supplies that cost them a lot of extra money, and if that is the case, you are doing object lessons the wrong

Object Lessons Out of Anything

way. Object lessons don't need to a long list of expensive supplies. You can use anything lying around your house or church and turn it into an effective object lesson kids will love. In fact, a more mundane item can be the most effective in an object lesson. For example, in one of our messages, we used three items kids would probably see or use every day: a pillow, a blanket, and ice cream. We talked about how we are blessed even when we mourn and are sad about something. We might turn to items like our favorite blanket, a nice pillow to cry on, and some good old-fashioned comfort food like ice cream to comfort us when we are sad. Even though those items can provide some temporary comfort for us, we have something or someone so much better than that who comforts us when we are sad. If we are Christians, we have the Holy Spirit living inside of us. The Bible tells us that the Holy Spirit is also our comforter. He will never leave us or forsake us.

Now, imagine the next time those kids cuddle up in a blanket, or lay their head down on a pillow. Those items will jog something in their memory, and they will be reminded that the Holy Spirit is their comforter. Always use items and examples that relate to the kids' lives in your object lessons. Jesus' teachings and parables were and still are awesome to learn from, but kids may need a more culturally relevant object lesson to drive home the point. They may not understand the concept of yeast spreading through a whole batch of dough or how small a mustard seed really is. Our challenge is to find items that kids are familiar with, so they can help them relate to the message in their own way.

Inspiration for object lessons can come from anywhere. If you are having a hard time finding inspiration, spend some time intentionally looking at the objects around you. Start in your own house. Walk around your house looking for items that kids and families in your ministry might also have in their homes. Gravitate toward favorite foods, pictures in frames, keepsake items, stuffed animals, pets, clothing, etc.

Spark

Make a list of those common household items and begin to brainstorm object lessons you could teach using those items. Some objects may give you more inspiration than others, but they should ultimately give you lots of different topics to work with. Write them all down with enough detail so you can come to the list for ideas later on.

If household items aren't giving you enough inspiration, step outside and spend some time in nature. Jesus loved to use objects and animals found in nature to teach people. Perhaps it was because He did a lot of His teaching outside in nature. I love to imagine Jesus teaching a crowd of people hungry to learn. As Jesus is teaching, He sees a group of birds flying overhead and He says, "Look at the birds. They don't plant or harvest or store food in barns, for your heavenly Father feeds them. And aren't you far more valuable to Him than they are? Can all your worries add a single moment to your life?" (Matthew 6:26-27 NLT) Then, Jesus notices the people are sitting in a field of grass filled with flowers and He says, "Look at the lilies of the field and how they grow. They don't work or make their clothing, yet Solomon in all his glory was not dressed as beautifully as they are. And if God cares so wonderfully for wildflowers that are here today and thrown into the fire tomorrow, He will certainly care for you. Why do you have so little faith?" (Matthew 6:28-30)

Jesus loved to use things in nature to help people understand His teachings. Nature is filled with examples of spiritual truths, and I don't think that is a coincidence. We can use the things God has provided in nature to teach kids today as well.

If you're still struggling with coming up with current and relevant object lessons, take a look at what's trending. If you don't know what's trending with kids in the age group you are teaching, spend some time figuring it out. We cannot effectively reach the kids we are ministering to without understanding what they like and dislike, and it's constantly changing. A fidget spinner might be trending one month and be out the next month. Being out of touch with culture and what's trending can hurt our credibility with the kids. Older kids are more likely to listen to us and be receptive to our messages when they know we care about what matters to them. Object lessons created around trends will have a shorter lifespan and may not have the ability to be re-used, but that doesn't mean you should avoid them all together. I have used slime, popular movies, video games, and clothing trends in object lessons. Kids love it when we incorporate trendy items into our messages, and their ears perk up when they hear a familiar subject come up.

Creativity Challenge

Let's have some fun and put your object lesson skills to the test! Take a look at the list of items you can find around your house. If you didn't make that list, do it now. Write each household item on a small piece of paper and put the pieces of paper in a bowl or small container. Test your creativity by pulling out an item at random and try to come up with an object lesson on the spot incorporating the item and a passage of Scripture. Do this every day for a week with a different item, and you'll see how you can create an object lesson out of anything!

_____
_____
_____
_____
_____
_____
_____
_____
_____
_____
_____
_____
_____
_____
_____
_____
_____
_____

chapter 10

HOW TO CHOOSE THE RIGHT CURRICULUM AND MAKE IT YOUR OWN

From the time I started working in children's ministry as a volunteer and after I became Children's Pastor myself, I have used many of the major curriculums on the market as well as beginning to write my own in the last three years. I've picked up on a lot of helpful tips for choosing the right curriculum for your ministry and personalizing it to your ministry style and the kids in your church. If you have shopped around for children's ministry curriculum recently, you might have noticed there are a lot of options out there. It can become overwhelming and exhausting downloading sample lessons and trying to find the perfect fit for your kids.

My first tip is found right in the title of this chapter- Always make it your own! Does this take extra time out of your week? Yes, but you can't expect any curriculum to be the perfect fit for your kids and your teaching style as is. Most people don't have the time to write their own curriculum, but they are able to carve out a couple extra hours per week to tweak something to be their own. Don't be tempted to use curriculum the way it comes because you are just too busy to adapt it. You know your kids and the culture of your church and area better than any curriculum writer.

For example, the lessons you choose may have been written in Atlanta, Georgia, and what may have been funny or effective for the kids there may not work for the kids in your area. Most curriculums provide one or two games for you to use each week, but that doesn't mean those games are going to work the way they are written for your group. You may need to make adjustments to fit the size or age of your group. Messages may need to be shortened or lengthened to fit the attention spans of the kids in your group. If you have mostly older kids, you may want to shoot for a 15-20 minute message. If you work in the younger kids' area, you may want to shorten a message down to 5-10 minutes or break up the message time into multiple segments to keep them from losing their attention.

Don't feel bad about throwing out the stuff you don't like! I like to call this "the fluff", and most curriculum has a lot of fluff you can cut out to make it fit your time slot. You don't have to use it all just because you paid for it. Even though it might sound a little crazy, even published curriculum can have errors and biblical inaccuracies. That's why it's always important to proofread every week. If something doesn't sound quite right, double check it yourself in the Bible. Even curriculum providers with editors make mistakes, so we shouldn't just assume it's all correct.

Next, it's critical that you make it relevant to what the kids are interested in right now. Some trends can last a few years while other trends may only last a few months. A while back, it would have been super relevant to use a curriculum themed around fidget spinners, but that trend was gone so fast that stores couldn't get rid of them. Don't depend on your curriculum to follow the trends and stay relevant even if it's brand new. Take personal responsibility for knowing what your kids are watching, listening to, playing, and interested in. You can still save money by using older curriculum that been out for a while, but take the time to update it and add what the kids are interested in right now.

Most importantly, make it biblical. It might seem like you shouldn't have to worry about this if you are using a curriculum created for children's ministry, but I have definitely found some curriculum lacking in this area. Some curriculum I've used has a lot of great content, tons of small group activities, great graphics, videos and multiple game options, but seems to be lacking in Scripture. If you are experiencing this problem with the curriculum you are using, add the Scripture in yourself. It's not that hard! The Bible is full of stories and verses for any topic you might be teaching on during a series. It's important to remember that church isn't supposed to be school. Kids can learn good virtues like how to be kind when they're in school, but we need to teach the verses and biblical stories that explain why we should be kind to others. God's Word is the best curriculum we could ever teach our kids. It is important that we use God's Word and have kids dig into it with us every single week. Your curriculum may include a good amount of Scripture, but doesn't go deep enough when explaining the biblical truths and apologetics behind them. If that is the case, do your own research and add the deeper content yourself.

Some people may believe that curriculum is in one of two quadrants. It is either biblically deep or a lot of fun, but not both. It doesn't have to be that way. Once you have made sure your curriculum is full of Scripture and biblically deep enough for the kids, you have to make it fun too. I have found that some curriculum are extremely biblical, but lacking in the fun department. It is proven that kids learn more when they are having fun, so we need to make fun a priority in our curriculum

Spark

as well. If your curriculum doesn't include any games or the games are falling flat, you can add games of your own or alter the games provided to give them more purpose. The Internet is full of fun and creative game ideas if you aren't great at coming up with game ideas yourself. Play games that either include everyone or engage the audience.

Games aren't the only way to add some fun to your curriculum. Some curriculums come with built-in theming you can use to change your environment so that everything ties in. If your curriculum doesn't provide theming for you, you can add it in yourself. When you add theming to your curriculum, you can tie it into the games, message, skits and your environments. Fun doesn't have to be a waste of time if you use it to help kids engage in God's Word and make them love coming to church.

Reaching the kids in our ministries today is a bit different than it was for the previous generations. The kids we're ministering to are part of Generation Z. People that are part of this generation find it very valuable to be a part of the learning process. They don't just want to be told what to do and what to believe, they want to be included in the process of figuring it out for themselves. It is crucial that we are making our services interactive and not just a one-way street of communication if we want to reach this generation. Kids don't want to be spectators watching a show when they come to our kids ministry services.

Now, most curriculum doesn't include response times and interaction in their large group portion, and while small group time may be interactive, we need to make sure our entire services are interactive for the kids. We need to involve them in any elements of the service we can. Look for opportunities to ask the kids questions as often as possible. Questions during skits and messages can include them and draw their attention back to what you're teaching. Use kids to help you share the Bible story or object lesson with the rest of the audience. Kids love volunteering to be a part of the service, and it never gets

How to Choose the Right Curriculum and Make it Your Own

old for them. If you are having a hard time keeping your kids' attention, try making your curriculum more interactive.

Lastly, make your curriculum easy for your team to use. Most of us aren't single-handedly running our ministries and using curriculum all by ourselves. We have a team of volunteers or leaders who teach and lead in multiple rooms every week, and we need that team to stick with us. Unfortunately, God did not give children's pastors the super-power of omnipresence, so we have to make our curriculum simple to use and easy to understand when we can't be in the room with our leaders. If your curriculum is forty pages printed out each week, you are going to want to simplify it and organize it so it can be used concisely, or your volunteers will become overwhelmed, confused, and discouraged.

One way to simplify this is to create a schedule for the morning in each classroom. Use this to organize the curriculum into smaller bits each volunteer needs to know and instructions on what they should use with the kids. I like using Planning Center Online because you can schedule your volunteers through it as well, but a simple Word document would work just as effectively. Put everything in the schedule and give your volunteers only what they need, not everything that is included in your curriculum. Yes, this requires more work on your part as the leader, but it ensures that your volunteers know what they are doing and you know they are teaching the most important parts.

It is important to remember that no curriculum will ever be exactly what you need as written, unless you have time to write it yourself. If you have been searching for that elusive, perfect curriculum that you can just print and hand to your volunteers, you might as well be looking for a pet unicorn because you won't find that anywhere. Even so, that doesn't necessarily mean you are already using the best curriculum for your ministry. Don't be afraid to look around and try something new for a change. Find a curriculum that is the best fit for you and your church's needs. There are many curriculums out there for a reason.

Spark

There isn't a one-size-fits-all option. Talk with your key volunteers to make sure they are enjoying the curriculum you are using as well. They may have some helpful suggestions for tweaking what you're currently using, or you may decide it's time for you to make a curriculum change. If they have concerns or questions about the curriculum you are using, be attentive and address them and make changes as needed. Curriculum will be one of your best and most helpful resources in your ministry if you take the time to make it your own, relevant, biblical, fun, interactive, and easy for your team to use.

Creativity Challenge

Print out a week of the curriculum you are using right now. Take the time to ask yourself these questions: How can I make this my own? How can I make this relevant to what the kids are into right now? How can make this more Biblical or add some Biblical depth to the content of the message? How can I make it more fun? How can I make the whole service more interactive? How can I make this easier for my team to prepare for and use? Once you have asked those questions, make the needed changes and ask some of your lead volunteers what they think about the changes you have made.

chapter 11

CREATING YOUR OWN CURRICULUM

AFTER READING THE LAST chapter and vetting your curriculum through all those qualifications, you might be ready to throw out your curriculum entirely and try your hand at creating your own. Maybe you have always wanted to write your own, but you don't know where to start. Creating your own curriculum is always an option if you are willing to put in the time and energy to make it happen week after week. Before we get down to the details on where to begin, let's talk about why a lot of people don't write their own. There is a lot of great curriculum on the market right now, and the prices vary enough that there is an option for every budget. There are quite a few free options that may need some more work on your part, but are a great place to start without having to write curriculum entirely from a blank page of paper. There are many curriculum providers that will offer discounts and scholarships to smaller churches with little or no budgets.

Spark

Many children's ministry leaders are part-time or volunteer, and they simply don't have enough time to write their own curriculum, plus they have way too many other things on their plate to spend that much time on curriculum preparation. Some leaders may think they aren't qualified to write their own curriculum because they don't have a degree in children's ministry and believe that curriculum providers are more qualified to create a comprehensive scope and sequence. It may surprise you to know that many of the curriculum providers don't have degrees either and may not be providing the most biblical content for your kids. Others may not think they are creative enough to write their own.

On the flip side, there are several reasons you might want to consider creating your own. If you aren't happy with the curriculum you have been using or you have looked around and don't like any of the options that fit in your budget, you might be feeling motivated to try writing it yourself. You might have realized that the number of hours you are spending every week tweaking and editing curriculum isn't worth the money you are spending on it. God might even be nudging you to step out of your comfort zone and create something new and fresh for the kids in your ministry. Perhaps your Lead Pastor would like you to align your curriculum with a sermon series he is doing in the main service, and you will need to go off curriculum and write something on your own to do so. One thing I know is that if God and/or your Lead Pastor are calling you to do something, you need to listen and act.

I began writing curriculum almost three years ago for a combination of some of the reasons I just mentioned. I had used a lot of the major curriculum providers out there and was never satisfied with any of them. I would spend hours upon hours editing, throwing fluff out, and adding biblical content to each of the curriculum I used, and I realized it wasn't worth the money I was spending on it. After changing ministry positions to a large church with a smaller budget than I had in

Creating Your Own Curriculum

my previous position, I wanted to make the most of the small budget I had and was tired of spending half of my budget on curriculum. One summer, my Lead Pastor announced that he would be preaching on a series entitled "Marvel" in the main service. The second I heard about that sermon series, I knew we had to do it with our kids as well. I knew the kids would love a superhero theme and the families in the church would love having the whole family on the same page for the summer. During those eight weeks of writing that series on my own, I felt God nudge me repeatedly to continue writing my own curriculum. I had never intended on writing my own material full time, but God had other plans for me. It has been hard at times to keep writing my own curriculum because it never ends, but I have continued to write it and have seen God bless our ministry through it.

Creating your own curriculum may or may not be for you, and it's definitely not for everyone. It is totally ok to keep using curriculum if that is working for you and your ministry, but always remember to make it your own. Even if you are not currently in a ministry season where writing your own curriculum is feasible, you may want to take a break from your usual and write a series or a stand-alone week at some point. Your Lead Pastor may even ask you to do a series with him, and you need to be ready to know how to write your own curriculum. If an opportunity or calling to create your material presents itself, you will need a process for getting from a blank sheet of paper to a full curriculum series. I will share my process for creating curriculum with you in this chapter. Feel free to use my process or adapt it to make it work for you.

When I first started writing curriculum, I had no plan, no process, I was just winging it. I didn't realize when I was writing that first series to go along with my Lead Pastor's sermon series that I was going to continue writing curriculum on a regular basis. My first few curriculum series still turned out ok, but over time, I began to develop a plan and a process for writing curriculum. I became more strategic in planning my series' as a whole instead of just writing each week as it came along. I even began planning out an entire year of curriculum series in advance, which I would highly recommend.

If you are planning on writing curriculum full time for the foreseeable future, you will need to spend even more time planning out what you are going to teach the kids. You will want to develop at least a one-year scope and sequence. Most curriculums now offer at least a one-year scope and sequence, but some may even offer as long as three years. At this point in the planning process, you only need to decide on the big picture items like themes (if desired), teaching topics, and Bible stories you want to cover. You will need to keep brainstorming ideas until you have a full year of curriculum ready to go. Since you are creating the curriculum, you get to decide if you want to be consistent and plan series that change every month, or if you want to switch things up. I like to have the flexibility of switching things up. I normally plan my series in 4, 6, 8, and even 12 week chunks. My preferred length of series is 6-8 weeks because it gives you and your team more time to settle into the theme and can save you money as well. Sometimes I throw in a stand-alone week between series to address important topics like baptism, communion, or worship. Writing your own curriculum gives you the flexibility to take your time and teach on what your kids really need to hear right now.

Once you have your scope and sequence laid out, you can begin writing your first curriculum series. There are three things I require out of each of my curriculum series: they should be fun, biblically deep, and easy for my team to use. At this point in the planning process, you will need to decide on the elements you want to include in each curriculum series. Most curriculum includes a large group and small group portion, so you may want to include those options in your agenda. Some elements you may want to include are: a series verse, weekly verses, skits, games, messages, object lessons, small group

Creating Your Own Curriculum

time, review questions, take-home cards, and service notes. It's your curriculum, so you can include only the elements you will actually use in your kids ministry.

Next, decide on the order you want the elements to go in and make an outline you will follow each week. Then, it's time to make some more brainstorming lists! I like to brainstorm each of the main elements in each series before I begin writing the weekly content. We use skits in our curriculum, so I create a brainstorming list for the skit including a character bio, storyline ideas, costume ideas, accents, and catch phrases for the character. I make a list of the Bible stories, teaching topics, Bible characters, and Scripture passages I would like to use in the messages. We always offer one large group game and one small group game every week. That means if a curriculum series is eight weeks long, I will need to have a list of at least eight large group games and eight small group games. Sometimes I come up with new games as I'm planning from week to week, and some of the games on the brainstorming list get thrown out. We love theming our environments to go along with the theme in our curriculum, so I create an environment's brainstorming list as well. I create a Pinterest board for each curriculum series beforehand and include game, message, and décor ideas to the board for added inspiration.

You are now ready to start writing your weekly content. Before you just begin writing, it is important to outline all of your elements for the week using the lists you created during your brainstorming session for the series. Now, you can begin filling in the smaller elements for each week which could include the weekly verse, small group questions, small group verses, review questions, takeaway statements, and other notes. I still like to use a paper and pen, so I like to do all my brainstorming lists and weekly outlines by hand. I use an iPad Pro, Apple Pencil, and Microsoft OneNote, and create a notebook for each curriculum series. I am still able to get the feeling that I'm writing on a piece of paper because I use the pencil to jot

Spark

down all of my lists and outlines. The great thing is I can access my notes anywhere on my phone, iPad, and computer, so I'm never without my notes when I need them. It will help you immensely with your week to week writing if you take the time to make a template you can use for each week.

Once you have the first week written, the other weeks are so much easier because you are simply filling in the template you created on the first week. It's finally time to start writing the weekly content of your curriculum. You can just make a simple, editable version of your curriculum in Word or Pages. It doesn't have to be fancy if you don't want it to be. After all, the kids will never see the written content for your curriculum, they will only experience it. As you write, remember to take each element from your weekly outline one at a time and don't get overwhelmed.

It's time to put the finishing touches on your curriculum. Kids are visually stimulated, and most learn better when more than one of their senses is being engaged. Most curriculum you buy will include at least some graphics and/or video content for you to use during your services. So what can you do to add these elements to your curriculum? Your church may already have a creative team in place who may be able to create graphics and videos for you. If not, you may be able to find someone in your church who is good at graphic design and have them create graphics for your curriculum based on your vision. If you can't find anyone to help you, there are free sites available, like Canva, which allow you to create your own simple graphics, take-home cards, and even a pretty curriculum template if you so desire. Canva is extremely user-friendly and anyone can learn how to make graphics for their own ministry using this free resource.

Although I don't believe videos are necessary for creating a quality curriculum that kids will enjoy, you can try your hand at making your own videos. You can use a free program like iMovie to create lyric videos and other videos for your

Creating Your Own Curriculum

ministry. Be aware that creating and editing videos can take up a lot of your time. Only you can decide if you need to include video content in your curriculum. Writing curriculum every week can seem daunting, but you will get better and faster each week you stick with it. When I first started writing curriculum, it would easily take me eight hours a week to write. Now, I can write a week of curriculum in under four hours and my writing has improved tremendously. Get out there and give creating your own curriculum a try. You may love it and never turn back. If you are interested in checking out my curriculum, you can find it at kidmincorinne.com.

Creativity Challenge

Pull out a piece of paper and a pen or a laptop if you prefer. Set a timer for fifteen minutes. During that time period, you will brainstorm your own curriculum series. Make sure you will have no interruptions during this time. Come up with as many elements as you can before the timer goes off. Come up with a theme, Bible stories/teaching topics to cover, how many weeks the series will be, a character idea, and game ideas. When the time is up, review your brainstorming list and see how much you were able to create during only fifteen minutes of uninterrupted time.

FINAL THOUGHTS

I HOPE YOU HAVE ENJOYED this book and I pray that it has sparked a new level of creativity in you that you never realized was there before. You may have felt empowered and ready to get out there and try something you have never done before, or you may have felt challenged or even discouraged by some of the chapters because it's "not in your wheel house."

I would encourage you to try something new, even if you don't feel like you are good at it. Allow yourself room for learning and be willing to fail. There is a lot to learn from our failures if we are open to what God wants to teach us through them. Creativity isn't just a natural trait some people are born with and others just don't have. Creativity can be learned and involves a lot of hard work in some areas. Your creative ceiling is only as high as you make it!

Don't forget to include God in your creativity process. I mentioned in the introduction that I always pray before I begin any new project. This is the most important step you can take in the process. If you need more creativity or a skill you don't have, ask God! God is the giver of all gifts, including creativity. He wants to equip you for the ministry He has called you to do. He wants to be a part of every event, game, set design, curriculum series, and idea you have. We must never get so caught up in our own plans and ideas that we forget to ask God what He wants to accomplish.

Spark

If you read this book quickly, I would encourage you to take the time to read it again at a slower pace. Allow yourself a week or even a month per chapter to allow the ideas to soak in. Give yourself the time to actually try out the creativity challenges at the end of each chapter. You aren't going to be able to accomplish all of the challenges in a week or a month, and you would make yourself crazy if you tried.

Books are only as useful as the action they inspire you to take to do something with the information you have just consumed. Don't skip over those challenges! They are meant to give you action steps to put the ideas you just read about into action. Some of the challenges will be harder than others for you. You won't reach a new level of creativity unless you are willing to push yourself out of your comfort zone. Find a ministry friend or a volunteer in your ministry and ask them to complete the challenges with you. This will make it a lot more fun and provide accountability for both of you in the process. Now, get out there and start creating!